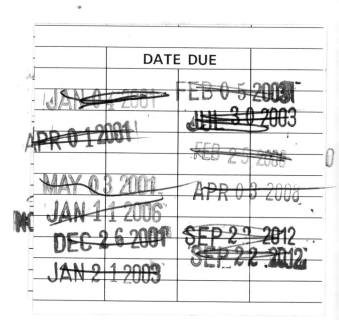

861
NER

Neruda, Pablo, 1904-
    1973.

The separate rose

DATE			

THE SEPARATE ROSE

La Rosa Separada

PABLO NERUDA

The Separate Rose

TRANSLATED BY WILLIAM O'DALY

COPPER CANYON PRESS : PORT TOWNSEND

Publication of this book was made possible by a grant from
the National Endowment for the Arts.
Copper Canyon Press is in residence with Centrum at
Fort Worden State Park.

ISBN 0-914742-88-4
Library of Congress Catalog Card Number 84-73338

The type is Sabon, set by Walker & Swenson, Book Typographers.
Cover image from the *Passport* series, oil on plexiglass,
by Galen Garwood.

Copper Canyon Press
Post Office Box 271
Port Townsend
Washington 98368

PREFACE

Easter Island, among inhabited islands, may be the most isolated in the world. Its high, basaltic mass rises from great depths in the South Pacific, 2,300 miles west of the Chilean coast. Three volcanic, grass-covered hills form the corners of the island's triangular shape. Sporadic clumps of shrubs and small trees are lost among oceanic grassland and lava flow which characterize the island. Its thirty-five miles of coastline are adorned with large, precisely cut stones that form altars (*ahu*), some ranging between one and two hundred yards in length. The altars serve as pedestals for the gigantic stone statues (*moai*), which the islanders carved during the centuries of isolation, and as burial sites for their ancestors. Many volcanic cones protrude from the grass-lands, one of them being Rano Raraku, inside whose crater gray, sixty-ton *moai* lie in various stages of completion. Finished statues twenty-five to thirty feet high dominate its slopes. Wind and flies sweep across the island. Striking sun-set hues suffuse the western coast, the low central hills and valleys, and cross over freshwater lakes in the craters. Thick mats of reeds prosper in these crater lakes, and bulrushes make the task of gathering water on the rocky island no easier.

Rapanui (as the people call the island and themselves) has been a possession of Chile since the late 19th Century. Pablo Neruda visited the island in 1971. The journey came at a particularly poignant time in the poet's life. Dying of

1

cancer, he was taking inventory of a lifetime of achievements and failures, and searching for enduring sources of hope amid the dreary political and social milieu. The mysterious island whetted Neruda's curiosity, mostly through the writings of Father Sebastian Englert, who during thirty-four years of missionary work had become its premier cultural historian. Neruda was aware that much of Rapanui's ancient history is unknown, and he knew that our limited understanding of the island's past had been gleaned primarily from tribal memory. Those sources narrate the story of the rise and decline of a tiny civilization, one whose life cycles resemble those of larger civilizations. By the late 1960s, Neruda had come to consider himself one member of a global civilization gone awry. He felt that the entire world was caught up in the trend of escalating national defense budgets at the expense of the human stomach and spirit. In response to the horror, we, like the tourists in Neruda's poem, continue to submerge ourselves in an endless cycle of acquiring and spending. That fatuous existence usurps our energies, and it successfully distracts us from the constant warfare, uprisings, feuds plaguing our planet. Even the temporary structures we inhabit allow us to forget the fragility of breath and blood. But the permanence of stone statues seduces and alarms our frightened souls.

Te Pito o Te Henua, Navel of the World, was one ancient name for the island. *Pito* and *henua* also strongly suggest center and uterus. From that island at the center of creation, a mythology unique to Rapanui has spread to every continent. In *The Separate Rose*, Neruda creates a mythology based on Rapanui sources. One legend says that the god Makemake made three attempts to create human beings. He fertilized a stone with his semen but nothing happened. Then he fertilized water, and the small fish called *paroko* were born. Finally he fertilized red earth, and a human being sprang to life. Neruda transforms Makemake into

2

"Lord Wind," who created all the islands of the sea. From his scattered sperm "was born the savage necklace of the myths." Wind shaped lava to beget the living statues that inhabit Rapanui.

> When the giants multiplied
> and walked tall and straight
> till they covered the island with stone noses
> and, so very alive, ordained their descendants: the children
> of wind and lava, the grandchildren
> of air and ash, they would stride
> on gigantic feet across their island:
> the breeze worked harder than ever
> with her hands,
> the typhoon with her crime,
> that persistence of Oceania.   (VII)

Neruda's sense of the island's purity recalls the Russian poet Osip Mandelstam's concept of stone: it is the offspring and the presence of the motion of wind and water. The earth itself is a place for building and burial, just as the stone altars function both as pedestals for the statues and as tombs for ancestors. The island and the *moai* were created out of the interaction of wind, water and lava. From Rapanui poured forth the potential for all creation, and there the secret of that birth remains hidden, surrounded by blue motion, clouds and stone.

Neruda knew that Rapanui was the last island in the Polynesian chain to be settled. Traditional sources speak of two groups of people which inhabited the island for much of its history. The Hanua Momoko and the Hanua Eepe shared the island in relative harmony for hundreds of years. They divided the island between them, the Momoko cultivating the territory of richest soil and the Eepe settling the rockier area which offered easy access to the sea. The

3

Momoko provided the Eepe with fruits, vegetables and scarce wood, while the Eepe distributed shellfish and the prized tuna. Though the two groups were competitive and occasionally feuded, intermarriage ensured their mutual desire for peaceful relations. During the peace, the two people's most outstanding achievement was the carving, transportation and erection of the stone figures.

The figures were meant to keep alive the memory of tribal ancestors. A population that probably never exceeded 4,000 carved almost 1,000 *moai*, and somehow transported them along prehistoric roads to the shoreline altars. The largest statue, Poro, weighs eighty-two tons and stands thirty-five feet tall. He was transported four miles from the crater workshop to his *ahu* at Anakena. Poro's topknot, worn like a hat, measures six feet high and seven feet in diameter, and weighs more than eleven tons. Master sculptors supervised the carving in the crater, and priests (*maori*) supervised the transportation of the finished statues. The sculptors were respected and paid handsomely in food. No slaves were involved in the long, tedious process of statue carving and conveyance. Apparently, both groups provided craftsmen and food to the cause.

Yet the stable relationship began to erode for reasons similar to those attributed by Paul Shepard, the cultural anthropologist, to Middle Eastern and European cultural declines. With the solving of the island's water collection problem and the refinement of agriculture, the population grew to unprecedented levels. The Little Ice Age in the 16th Century ushered in long decades cursed with poor harvests and mediocre fishing. Subsequent food shortages encouraged greed and pride; the need for power and protection provoked widespread feuding and one major war. The carving and transportation of the *moai* came to an abrupt halt. European explorers who visited the island in the 18th and 19th Centuries observed numerous statues strewn along overgrown roads and toppled from their *ahu*. Some figures were lying unfinished in the crater Rano Raraku, and full-sized *moai* lay fallen on its slopes.

Neruda had lived and worked among refugees from various colonizing raids. As a child, he had become familiar with the pride and pain of the Mapuche people, who lived near the frontier town of Temuco, where Neruda was raised. He knew the terror of European refugees whom he had assisted in fleeing Paris for Santiago during World War II. In modern history, the Rapanui had felt the effects of colonization. When the Dutchman Jacob Roggeveen sailed his three ships near the island on Easter morning, 1722, he named it in honor of the Christian world and opened the door for colonizers and slavers who eventually would follow. Roggeveen's well-armed crew members were jittery in their rowboats and sloops as they approached the pink sands of Anakena, home of the giant, Poro. Their muskets were poised and ready. A throng of Rapanui continued to assemble on the beach. Crew members panicked when an inquisitive Rapanui appeared to threaten them. They fired into the crowd, killing several islanders. Nevertheless, the Dutchmen were allowed to disembark. After a brief tour around the island, they departed with gifts of pineapple and sugar cane. In their hands the Rapanui weighed gifts of blue beads and mirrors.

Between 1858 and 1863, Peruvian slave ships carried away about 1,500 islanders, devastating the traditional way of life. Strange diseases took their toll of the Rapanui as well. Yet, traditional beliefs endure. Modern Rapanui believe that spirits inhabit remote areas of the island; sometimes they come as close as the limits of Hangoroa, the only village. By and large, the Rapanui still share the island with their supernatural beings, as the statues share it with Lord Wind in Neruda's mythos. To Neruda, it is essential that a people live with the gods who link them to their origins and

5

their truth. Life then becomes a form of praise and an act of faith, a binding force.

> here on Easter Island where everything is altar,
> where everything is a workroom for the unknown,
> a woman nurses her newborn
> upon the same steps that her gods tread.   (IX)

The alternative is to live estranged from ourselves and the earth, to be alone in one another's arms and separated from our souls. We spend our lives acquiring oblivion, and avoid contemplating the sources of our impoverished pathos. We put on different faces and keep moving to avoid seeing contradictions in our lives. In hotels, we put on our last clean shirt, and "on the edge of panic, pompous...we are one and the same" in the eyes of solitude and time. We wear the same thirsty skin, the same hair "only in different colors."

Just as in *Still Another Day* (*Aún*), Neruda identifies himself with the colonizers, "with the egalitarian tourists and their offspring." No longer are the poet's vision and desire for moral rectitude enough to absolve his guilt by association with the human world, as they were for the younger poet of *The Heights of Macchu Picchu* in 1945. (His own country had annexed Easter Island largely for strategic purposes.) But in *The Separate Rose*, the reader senses compassion in lines resonant with anguish and anger at our inability to make peace with ourselves, each other, and the earth. The poet's visit to Easter Island coincided with the large strikes which erupted in Chile after Presidente Salvador Allende took office. The United States was maneuvering for an overthrow of the freely elected Allende, and the Vietnam War raged on. Although Neruda fought throughout his lifetime for goals inspired by seemingly inex-

6

haustible hope, in *The Separate Rose* he fails to find the link between the mythological and natural purity of Rapanui and the human duplicity that has caught up our single destiny in its wave.

Neruda's inability to find a resolution is reflected in the book's musical structure. Composed as a long poem, it is written in two alternating voices, one of "The Island" and the other of "Men." The lines in the latter voice are often staccato, with hard masculine rhymes and multi-syllabic words which impede the flow. The voice laments the sadness of lives.

> turistas convencidos de volver, compañeros
> de calle negra con casas de anteqüedades
> y lato de basura, hermanastros
> del número treinta y tres mil cuatrocientos veintisiete,
> piso sexto, departamento a, be o jota... (X)

In the former voice we hear more feminine endings and sometimes startling compression and clarity. The love and longing Neruda felt for the island's purity is evident in these lines.

> oh estrella natural, diadema verde,
> sola en tu solitaria dinastía,
> inalcanzable aún, evasiva, desierta
> como una gota, como una uva, como el mar. (XVII)

Some passages are celebrations of the island's secret. In homage to Rano Raraku's creative mystery, the poet involves Villarrica in lines which express the dignity, fear and awe which seized him in the presence of that steaming Andean volcano of his childhood. In this powerful book, Neruda achieves nearly perfect sonal control.

La rosa separada was his second book to be posthumously published, one of eight which lay on his desk on the day of his death in September 1973. It belongs to the family of book-length poems most obviously begun with the publication of *Aún* in 1969. Beginning with that distillation of Neruda's lifelong themes and reading through the thirteen books of poems that follow it, the aficionado will marvel at the poet's range of expression. Don Pablo was a generous spirit. After reading other later books as diverse as *Jardín de invierno* (1974) and *Libro de las preguntas* (1974), we may again be convinced that the Nobel laureate has earned his place as one of the most eminent and necessary poets in any language.

WILLIAM O'DALY
APRIL 1985

ACKNOWLEDGMENTS

From the sources I consulted for information on Easter Island, I enthusiastically recommend the writings of Father Sebastian Englert, William Mulloy, and Grant McCall, all of whom have lived on the island and made it a major focus of their work. These authors treat the subject of Rapanui with great sensitivity and respect. Steven White, poet and translator of Latin American poetry, offered many insightful suggestions and comments which benefited the translations. And for his warm encouragement I thank Sergio Bocaz-Moraga, Professor of Modern Languages at Eastern Washington University. The criticisms and faith of a few good friends also helped to complete the process of bringing the poem into the American language. Perhaps in sharing the task, we have translated Pablo Neruda's generous spirit into our lives.

W. O'D.

THE SEPARATE ROSE

La Rosa Separada

INTRODUCCION

EN MI TEMA

A la Isla de Pascua y las presencias
salgo, saciado de puertas y calles,
a buscar algo que allí no perdí.
El mes de Enero, seco,
se parece a una espiga:
cuelga de Chile su luz amarilla
hasta que el mar lo borra
y yo salgo otra vez a regresar.

Estatuas que la noche construyó
y desgranó en un círculo cerrado
para que no las viera sino el mar.

(Viajé a recuperarlas, a erigirlas
en mi domicilio desaparecido.)

Y aquí rodeado de presencias grises,
de blancura espacial, de movimiento
azul, agua marina, nubes, piedra,
recomienzo las vidas de mi vida.

INTRODUCTION

MY THEMES

To Easter Island and the presences
I set out, fed up with doorways and streets,
to search for something I never lost there.
The month of January, so dry,
it resembles a spike of wheat:
its golden light hangs from Chile
until the sea washes it away
and I leave only to come back again.

Statues that night raised
and threshed in a closed circle
so the ocean alone would see them.

(I traveled there to recover them, to erect them
in my house that has vanished.)

And here, surrounded by grey presences,
by whiteness of space, by blue motion,
by sea water, clouds, stone,
I begin the lives of my life again.

I

LOS HOMBRES

Yo soy el peregrino
de Isla de Pascua, el caballero
extraño, vengo a golpear las puertas del silencio:
uno más de los que trae el aire
saltándose en un vuelo todo el mar:
aquí estoy, como los otros pesados peregrinos
que en inglés amamantan y levantan las ruinas:
egregios comensales del turismo, iguales a Simbad
y a Cristóbal, sin más descubrimiento
que la cuenta del bar.
                    Me confieso: matamos
los veleros de cinco palos y carne agusanada,
matamos los libros pálidos de marinos menguantes,
nos trasladamos en gansos inmensos de aluminio,
correctamente sentados, bebiendo copas ácidas,
descendiendo en hileras de estómagos amables.

I

MEN

I am the pilgrim
of Easter Island, the strange
knight, come to knock on the doors of silence:
one more of those brought by the air,
the whole sea leaping into flight:
I am here, like the other fat pilgrims
who in English suckle and raise the ruins:
illustrious courtiers of tourism, just like Sinbad
and Columbus, those who discover nothing more
than the price of their drinks.
                              I confess: we murdered
the five-masted ships and wormy meat,
we murdered the colorless books about sailors waning,
we transport ourselves in enormous aluminum geese,
seated correctly, drinking sour cocktails,
descending in rows of friendly stomachs.

II

LOS HOMBRES

Es la verdad del prólogo. Muerte al romanticón,
al experto en las incomunicaciones:
soy igual a la profesora de Colombia,
al rotario de Filadelfia, al comerciante
de Paysandú que juntó plata
para llegar aquí. Llegamos de calles diferentes,
de idiomas desiguales, al Silencio.

II

MEN

The truth is in the prologue. Death to the romantic fool,
to the expert in solitary confinement,
I'm the same as the teacher from Columbia,
the Rotarian from Philadelphia, the merchant
from Paysandu who saved his silver
to come here. We all arrive by different streets,
by unequal languages, at Silence.

LA ISLA

Antigua Rapa Nui, patria sin voz,
perdónanos a nosotros los parlanchines del mundo
hemos venido de todas partes a escupir en tu lava,
llegamos llenos de conflictos, de divergencias, de sangre,
de llanto y digestiones, de guerras y duraznos,
en pequeñas hileras de inamistad, de sonrisas
hipócritas, reunidos por los dados del cielo
sobre la mesa de tu silencio.

Una vez más llegamos a mancillarte.

Saludo primero al cráter, a Ranu Raraku, a sus párpados
de légamo, a sus viejos labios verdes:
es ancho, y altos muros lo circulan, lo encierran,
pero el agua allá abajo, mezquina, sucia, negra,
vive, se comunica con la muerte
como una iguana inmóvil, soñolienta, escondida.

Yo, aprendiz de volcanes, conocí,
infante aún, las lenguas de Aconcagua,
el vómito encendido del volcán Tronador,
en la noche espantosa vi caer
la luz del Villarrica fulminando las vacas,
torrencial, abrasando plantas y campamentos,
crepitar derribando peñascos en la hoguera.

Pero si aquí me hubiera dejado mi infancia,
en este volcán muerto hace mil años,

III

THE ISLAND

Ancient Rapa Nui, motherland without a voice,
forgive us, we ceaseless talkers of the world
come from all corners and spit in your lava,
we arrive full of conflicts, arguments, blood,
weeping and indigestion, wars and peach trees,
in small rows of soured friendships, of hypocritical
smiles, brought together by the sky's dice
upon the table of your silence.

Once more we've come to dishonor you.

I greet first the crater, Ranu Raraku, with its eyelids
of slime and old green lips:
it is wide, high walls circle it, enclose it,
but there below, the water, treacherous, filthy, black,
lives on, converses with death
like an immobile iguana, drowsy, hidden.

As apprentice to volcanoes, I knew
even as an infant the languages of Aconcagua,
the smoldering vomit of the volcano Tronador,
in the terrifying night I saw the light
from Villarica illuminate a herd of cows,
torrential, scorching the plants and campsites;
crackling, demolishing boulders in its blaze.

But if my childhood had abandoned me here,
in this volcano dead for a thousand years,

en este Ranu Raraku, ombligo de la muerte,
habría aullado de terror y habría obedecido:
habría deslizado mi vida en silencio,
hubiera caído al miedo verde, a la boca del cráter desdentado,
transformándome en légamo, en lenguas de la iguana.

Silencio depositado en la cuenca, terror
de la boca lunaria, hay un minuto, una hora
pesada como si el tiempo detenido
se fuera a convertir en piedra inmensa:
es un momento, pronto
también disuelve el tiempo su nueva estatua imposible
y queda el día inmóvil, como un encarcelado
dentro del cráter, dentro de la cárcel del cráter,
adentro de los ojos de la iguana del cráter.

in this Ranu Raraku, navel of death,
I would've howled in terror and obeyed:
my life would have slipped into silence
had I fallen into the green fear, into the mouth
                              of the toothless crater
and turned into slime, into languages of the iguana.

Silence deposited in the basin, what the mouth
in moonlight fears most. There's a minute, an hour
as heavy as time ground to a halt
and changed into a gigantic stone:
here one moment lives, and just as fast
time dissolves its impossible new statue:
and the day remains immobile, like a prisoner
inside the crater, inside the prison of the crater,
inside the eyes of the crater's iguana.

IV

LOS HOMBRES

Somos torpes los transeúntes, nos atropellamos de codos,
de pies, de pantalones, de maletas,
bajamos del tren, del jet, de la nave, bajamos
con arrugados trajes y sombreros funestos.
Somos culpables, somos pecadores,
llegamos de hoteles estancados o de la paz industrial,
ésta es tal vez la última camisa limpia,
perdimos la corbata,
pero aun así, desquiciados, solemnes,
hijos de puta considerados en los mejores ambientes,
o simples taciturnos que no debemos nada a nadie,
somos los mismos y lo mismo frente al tiempo,
frente a la soledad: los pobres hombres
que se ganaron la vida y la muerte trabajando
de manera normal o burotrágica,
sentados o hacinados en las estaciones del metro,
en los barcos, las minas, los centros de estudio, las cárceles,
las universidades, las fábricas de cerveza,
(debajo de la ropa la misma piel sedienta),
(el pelo, el mismo pelo, repartido en colores).

IV

MEN

We are the clumsy passersby, we push past each other with elbows,
with feet, with trousers, with suitcases,
we get off the train, the jet plane, the ship, we step down
in our wrinkled suits and sinister hats.
We are all guilty, we are all sinners,
we come from dead-end hotels or industrial peace,
this might be our last clean shirt,
we have misplaced our tie,
yet even so, on the edge of panic, pompous,
sons of bitches who move in the highest circles
or quiet types who don't owe anything to anybody,
we are one and the same, the same in time's eyes,
or in solitude's: we are the poor devils
who earn a living and a death working
bureautragically or in the usual ways,
sitting down or packed together in subway stations,
boats, mines, research centers, jails,
universities, breweries,
(under our clothes the same thirsty skin),
(the hair, the same hair, only in different colors).

V

LA ISLA

Todas las islas del mar las hizo el viento.

Pero aquí, el coronado, el viento vivo, el primero,
fundó su casa, cerró las alas, vivió:
desde la mínima Rapa Nui repartió sus dominios,
sopló, inundó, manifestó sus dones
hacia el Oeste, hacia el Este, hacia el espacio unido
hasta que estableció gérmenes puros,
hasta que comenzaron las raíces.

V

THE ISLAND

The wind created all the islands of the sea.

But here, the exalted one, the Overlord, the living wind,
established his home, folded his wings, reigned:
from humble Rapa Nui he parceled out his dominion,
he blew, he poured forth, he showered us with gifts,
to the west, to the east, in the smooth curve of space
until the purest buds appeared,
until roots were born.

VI

LA ISLA

Oh Melanesia, espiga poderosa,
islas del viento genital, creadas,
luego multiplicadas por el viento.

De arcilla, bosques, barro, de semen que volaba
nació el collar salvaje de los mitos:
Polinesia: pimienta verde, esparcida
en el área del mar por los dedos errantes
del dueño de Rapa Nui, el Señor Viento.

La primera estatua fue de arena mojada,
él la formó y la deshizo alegremente.
La segunda estatua la construyó de sal
y el mar hostil la derribó cantando.
Pero la tercera estatua que hizo el Señor Viento
fue un moai de granito, y éste sobrevivió.

Esta obra que labraron las manos del aire,
los guantes del cielo, la turbulencia azul,
este trabajo hicieron los dedos transparentes:
un torso, la erección del Silencio desnudo,
la mirada secreta de la piedra,
la nariz triangular del ave o de la proa
y en la estatua el prodigio de un retrato:
porque la soledad tiene este rostro,
porque el espacio es esta rectitud sin rincones,
y la distancia es esta claridad del rectángulo.

THE ISLAND

O Melanesia, powerful spike of wheat,
islands of genital wind, created
then multiplied by the wind

From clay, forests, mud, from scattered sperm
was born the savage necklace of the myths:
Polynesia, green pepper, broadcast over
the surface of the sea by the wandering fingers
of the master of Rapa Nui, Lord Wind.

The first statue was made of damp sand,
he shaped it and gladly destroyed it.
He made the second statue out of salt
and hostile seas demolished it, singing.
But the third statue that Lord Wind carved
was a *moai* of granite, and this one survived.

This piece was polished by hands of air,
gloves of sky, the blue turbulence,
this work was finished by transparent fingers:
a torso, the erection of naked silence,
the mysterious look of stone,
the triangular nose of the bird or of the prow
and in the statue the miracle of this portrait:
because solitude wears this face,
because space stands plumb without corners,
and distance has the clarity of a rectangle.

VII

LA ISLA

Cuando prolificaron los colosos
y erguidos caminaron
hasta poblar la isla de narices de piedra
y, activos, destinaron descendencia: hijos
del viento y de la lava, nietos
del aire y la ceniza, recorrieron
con grandes pies la isla:
nunca trabajó tanto
la brisa con sus manos,
el ciclón con su crimen,
la persistencia de la Oceanía.

Grandes cabezas puras,
altas de cuello, graves de mirada,
gigantescas mandíbulas erguidas
en el orgullo de su soledad,
presencias,
presencias arrogantes,
preocupadas.

Oh graves dignidades solitarias
¿quién se atrevió, se atreve
a preguntar, a interrogar
a las estatuas interrogadoras?

Son la interrogación diseminada
que sobrepasa la angostura exacta,
la pequeña cintura de la isla

VII

THE ISLAND

When the giants multiplied
and walked tall and straight
till they covered the island with stone noses
and, so very alive, ordained their descendents: the children
of wind and lava, the grandchildren
of air and ash, they would stride
on gigantic feet across their island:
the breeze worked harder than ever
with her hands,
the typhoon with her crime,
that persistence of Oceania.

Great pure heads,
tall necks, grave faces,
their immense square jaws
prideful in their solitude,
presences,
arrogant presences,
troubled.

O solemn nobles so alone
who dared, who dares
to interrogate, to question
the inquisitive statues?

They are a question that scatters,
that sails beyond this exact narrowness,
this small belt of island

y se dirige al grande mar, al fondo
del hombre y de su ausencia.

Algunos cuerpos no alcanzaron a erguirse:
sus brazos se quedaron sin forma aún, sellados
en el cráter, durmientes,
acostados aún en la rosa calcárea,
sin levantar los ojos hacia el mar
y las grandes criaturas de sueño horizontal
son las larvas de piedra del misterio:
aquí las dejó el viento cuando huyó de la tierra:
cuando dejó de procrear hijos de lava.

toward the vast ocean, the depths
of man and of his absence.

Some figures weren't able to raise themselves up:
their arms still unformed, they were sealed
inside the crater, asleep,
still lying in the calcareous rose,
not lifting their eyes toward the sea
and the great creatures sleeping on the horizon
are the stone larvae of mystery:
the wind left them here when the wind fled the earth
and no longer begot children of lava.

VIII

LA ISLA

Los rostros derrotados en el centro,
quebrados y caídos, con sus grandes narices
hundidas en la costra calcárea de la isla,
¿los gigantes indican a quién? ¿a nadie?
un camino, un extraño camino de gigantes:
allí quedaron rotos cuando avanzaron, cayeron
y allí quedó su peso prodigioso caído,
besando la ceniza sagrada, regresando
al magma natalicio, malheridos, cubiertos
por la luz oceánica, la corta lluvia, el polvo
volcánico, y más tarde
por esta soledad del ombligo del mundo:
la soledad redonda de todo el mar reunido.

Parece extraño ver vivir aquí, dentro
del círculo, contemplar las langostas
róseas, hostiles caer a los cajones
desde las manos de los pescadores,
y éstos, hundir los cuerpos otra vez en el agua
agrediendo las cuevas de su mercadería,
ver las viejas zurcir pantalones gastados
por la pobreza, ver entre follajes

la flor de una doncella sonriendo a sí misma,
al sol, al mediodía tintineante,
a la iglesia del padre Englert, allí enterrado,
sí, sonriendo, llena de esta dicha remota
como un pequeño cántaro que canta.

VIII

THE ISLAND

Defeated faces in the center,
cracked and fallen, with their great noses
sunk in the calcareous crust of the island,
these giants point to whom? to no one?
a road, a strange road of giants:
they stopped here, having shattered as they advanced,
and here forever their enormous masses lie fallen,
kissing the sacred ash, returning
to the natal magma, mortally wounded, shrouded
in oceanic light, brief rain, volcanic
dust, and later
by the loneliness of the world's navel:
the circular solitude of the whole sea, united.

It seems strange to find life there, inside
the circle, to think about the rosy
lobsters, hostile as they fall into crates
from the hands of the fishermen,
and these men, who plunge their bodies into the ocean
that assaults the caves containing their harvest,
to watch the old women mending trousers worn thin
by poverty, to see among the dense leaves

the flower of a virgin smiling at herself,
at the sun, at the tiny bells of noon,
at the church of Father Englert, buried there,
and yes, smiling, full of this distant happiness
like a small wine pitcher that sings.

IX

LOS HOMBRES

A nosotros nos enseñaron a respetar la iglesia,
a no toser, a no escupir en el atrio,
a no lavar la ropa en el altar
y no es así: la vida rompe las religiones
y es esta isla en que habitó el Dios Viento
la única iglesia viva y verdadera:
van y vienen las vidas, muriendo y fornicando:
aquí en la Isla de Pascua donde todo es altar,
donde todo es taller de lo desconocido,
la mujer amamanta su nueva criatura
sobre las mismas gradas que pisaron sus dioses.

¡Aquí, a vivir! ¿Pero también nosotros?
Nosotros, los transeúntes, los equivocados de estrella,
naufragaríamos en la isla como en una laguna,
en un lago en que todas las distancias concluyen,
en la aventura inmóvil más difícil del hombre.

IX

MEN

They taught us to respect the church,
not to cough, not to spit in the atrium,
not to wash our clothes upon the altar,
but it's not so: life tears apart religions,
and on this island the Wind God inhabits
the only church living and true:
our lives come and go, dying, making love:
here on Easter Island where everything is altar,
where everything is a workroom for the unknown,
a woman nurses her newborn
upon the same steps that her gods tread.

Here, they live! But do we?
We transients, followers of the wrong star,
were shipwrecked on this island as in a lagoon,
like in a lake in which all distances end,
on a motionless journey, so difficult for men.

X

LOS HOMBRES

Sí, próximos desengañados, antes de regresar
al redil, a la colmena de las tristes abejas,
turistas convencidos de volver, compañeros
de calle negra con casas de antigüedades
y latas de basura, hermanastros
del número treinta y tres mil cuatrocientos veintisiete,
piso sexto, departamento a, be o jota
frente al almacén "Astorquiza, Williams y Compañía"
sí, pobre hermano mío que eres yo,
ahora que sabemos que no nos quedaremos
aquí, ni condenados, que sabemos
desde hoy, que este esplendor nos queda grande,
la soledad nos aprieta como el traje de un niño
que crece demasiado o como cuando
la oscuridad se apodera del día.

X

MEN

Yes, soon they'll see where they went wrong, before returning
to the flock, to the hive of sad bees,
these tourists convinced they'll soon be back, the ones
who share the black street and live in houses full of antiques
and garbage pails, stepbrothers
in room thirty-three thousand four hundred twenty-seven,
sixth floor, apartment A, B or J,
facing the warehouse of Astorquiza, Williams and Company,
yes, my poor brother, we're one and the same,
now that we realize we can never stay
here, not even in jail; as of today we know
that this grandeur is too big for us,
that solitude crowds us like a little boy's suit
who has grown too fast, or the way
darkness embraces the day.

XI

LOS HOMBRES

Se ve que hemos nacido para oírnos y vernos,
para medirnos (cuánto saltamos, cuánto ganamos,
                          ganamos, etcétera),
para ignorarnos (sonriendo), para mentirnos,
para el acuerdo, para la indiferencia or para
comer juntos.
Pero que no nos muestre nadie la tierra, adquirimos
olvido, olvido hacia los sueños de aire,
y nos quedó sólo un regusto de sangre y polvo
en la lengua: nos tragamos el recuerdo
entre vino y cerveza, lejos, lejos de aquello,
lejos de aquello, de la madre, de la tierra de la vida.

XI

MEN

One can see we were born to hear and see each other,
to compete (how high we jump, how often we win, how much
                we earn, et cetera),
to ignore each other (smiling), to lie
in order to agree or be indifferent or eat together.
But let no one reveal the world to us, for we acquire
oblivion, nothing but dreams of air,
and all that's left is an aftertaste of blood and dust
on the tongue: we swallow the memory
with wine and beer, so far, far from all that,
from the mother, from the land of our lives.

XII

LA ISLA

Austeros perfiles de cráter labrado, narices
en el triángulo, rostros de dura miel,
silenciosas campanas cuyo sonido
se fue hacia el mar para no regresar, mandíbulas, miradas
de sol inmóvil, reino
de la gran soledad, vestigios
verticales:
yo soy el nuevo, el oscuro,
soy de nuevo el radiante:
he venido tal vez a relucir,
quiero el espacio ígneo
sin pasado, el destello,
la oceanía, la piedra y el viento
para tocar y ver, para construir de nuevo,
para solicitar de rodillas la castidad del sol,
para cavar con mis pobres manos sangrientas el destino.

THE ISLAND

Severe profiles from the carved crater, noses
in the shape of a triangle, faces of hardened honey,
silent bells whose sound
went out to sea and never returned, jawbones, the look
of the motionless sun, kingdom
of the vast solitude, vertical
ruins:
I am the new one, an unknown,
I glow with new radiance:
perhaps I've come to shine,
I want the igneous space
without a past, that sparkle,
I want to touch, to know Oceania,
stone and wind, to build and build again,
to court on my knees the chastity of the sun,
to dig out my destiny with poor bloody hands.

XIII

LOS HOMBRES

Llegamos hasta lejos, hasta lejos
para entender las órbitas de piedra,
los ojos apagados que aún siguen mirando,
los grandes rostros dispuestos para la eternidad.

XIII

MEN

We went a long way, a long way
to understand the orbits of stone,
the extinguished eyes still gazing out,
the gigantic faces ready to enter eternity.

XIV

LOS HOMBRES

Qué lejos, lejos, lejos continuamos,
nos alejamos de las duras máscaras
erigidas en pleno silencio y nos iremos
envueltos en su orgullo, en su distancia.

¿Y para qué vinimos a la isla?
No será la sonrisa de los hombres floridos,
ni las crepitantes caderas de Ataroa la bella,
ni los muchachos a caballo, de ojos impertinentes,
lo que nos llevaremos regresando:
sino un vacío oceánico, una pobre pregunta
con mil contestaciones de labios desdeñosos.

XIV

MEN

Such a long, long way we have to go,
even farther from the stone masks
standing erect, in utter silence, and we'll go
wrapped in their pride, in their distance.

What brought us to the island?
It won't be the smile of flowering men,
or the crackling waist of lovely Ataroa,
or the boys on horseback, with their rude eyes,
that we'll take home with us:
just an oceanic emptiness, a poor question
with a thousand answers on contemptuous lips.

XV

LOS HOMBRES

El transeúnte, viajero, el satisfecho,
vuelve a sus ruedas a rodar, a sus aviones,
y se acabó el silencio solemne, es necesario
dejar atrás aquella soledad transparente
de aire lúcido, de agua, de pasto duro y puro,
huir, huir, huir de la sal, del peligro,
del solitario círculo en el agua
desde donde los ojos huecos del mar,
las vértebras, los párpados de las estatuas negras
mordieron al espantado burgués de las ciudades:

Oh Isla de Pascua, no me atrapes,
hay demasiada luz, estás muy lejos,
y cuánta piedra y agua:
too much for me! ¡Nos vamos!

XV

MEN

The transient, the smug traveler, returns
to his wheels ready to roll, to his jet planes,
and the deep silence ends, he must leave
behind the transparent solitude
of thin air, of water, of pastureland rugged and pure,
to escape, to escape, to flee the salt and peril,
that lonely circle in the water
where the hollow eyes of the sea,
the vertebrae, the eyelids of the black statues
chewed at the frightened bourgeois from the cities:

O Easter Island, do not seize me,
the light is too bright, you are so distant
and so much stone and water:
"too much for me!" Let's get out of here!

XVI

LOS HOMBRES

El fatigado, el huérfano
de las multitudes, el yo,
el triturado, el del cemento,
el apátrida de los restaurantes repletos,
el que quería irse más lejos, siempre,
no sabía qué hacer en la isla, quería
y no quería quedarse o volver,
el vacilante, el híbrido, el enredado en sí mismo
aquí no tuvo sitio: la rectitud de piedra,
la mirada infinita del prisma de granito,
la soledad redonda lo expulsaron:
se fue con sus tristezas a otra parte,
regresó a sus natales agonías,
a las indecisiones del frío y del verano.

XVI

MEN

The weary one, orphan
of the masses, the self,
the crushed one, the one made of concrete,
the one without a country in crowded restaurants,
he who wanted to go far away, always farther away,
didn't know what to do there, whether he wanted
or didn't want to leave or remain on the island,
the hesitant one, the hybrid, entangled in himself,
had no place here: the straight-angled stone,
the infinite look of the granite prism,
the circular solitude all banished him:
he went somewhere else with his sorrows,
he returned to the agony of his native land,
to his indecisions, of winter and summer.

XVII

LA ISLA

Oh torre de la luz, triste hermosura
que dilató en el mar estatuas y collares,
ojo calcáreo, insignia del agua extensa, grito
de petrel enlutado, diente del mar, esposa
del viento de Oceanía, oh rosa separada
del tronco del rosal despedazado
que la profundidad convirtió en archipiélago,
oh estrella natural, diadema verde,
sola en tu solitaria dinastía,
inalcanzable aún, evasiva, desierta
como una gota, como una uva, como el mar.

XVII

THE ISLAND

O tower of light, sad beauty
that magnified necklaces and statues in the sea,
calcareous eye, insignia of the vast waters, cry
of the mourning petrel, tooth of the sea, wife
of the Oceanian wind, O separate rose
from the long stem of the trampled bush
that the depths converted into archipelago,
O natural star, green diadem,
alone in your lonesome dynasty,
still unattainable, elusive, desolate
like one drop, like one grape, like the sea.

XVIII

LOS HOMBRES

Como algo que sale del agua, algo desnudo, invicto,
párpado de planito, crepitación de sal,
alga, pez tembloroso, espada viva,
yo, fuera de los otros, me separo
de la isla separada, me voy
envuelto en luz
y si bien pertenezco a los rebaños,
a los que entran y salen en manadas,
al turismo igualitario, a la prole,
confieso mi tenaz adherencia al terreno
solicitado por la aurora de Oceanía.

XVIII

MEN

Like something rising from the water, something naked, invincible,
flat smooth eyelid, crackle of salt,
seaweed, quivering fish, living sword,
I, who left the others, who separated himself
on this separate island, now leave
wrapped in light
and if I do belong with the flocks,
with those beings who come and go in herds,
with the egalitarian tourists and their offspring,
I want my human roots to cling to the land
lured by an Oceanian dawn.

XIX

LOS HOMBRES

Volvemos apresurados a esperar nombramientos,
exasperantes publicaciones, discusiones amargas,
fermentos, guerras, enfermedades, música
que nos ataca y nos golpea sin tregua,
entramos a nuestros batallones de nuevo,
aunque todos se unían para declararnos muertos:
aquí estamos otra vez con nuestra falsa sonrisa,
dijimos, exasperados ante el posible olvido,
mientras allá en la isla sin palmeras,
allá donde se recortan las narices de piedra
como triángulos trazados a pleno cielo y sal,
allí, en el minúsculo ombligo de los mares,
dejamos olvidada la última pureza,
el espacio, el asombro de aquellas compañías
que levantan su piedra desnuda, su verdad,
sin que nadie se atreva a amarlas, a convivir con ellas,
y ésa es mi cobardía, aquí doy testimonio:
no me sentí capaz sino de transitorios
edificios, y en esta capital sin paredes
hecha de luz, de sal, de piedra y pensamiento,
como todos miré y abandoné asustado
la limpia claridad de la mitología,
las estatuas rodeadas por el silencio azul.

XIX

MEN

We dash back to sit and wait for diplomatic appointments,
exasperating publications, bitter feuds,
uprisings, wars, diseases, music
that attacks and hammers us without truce,
to march forth in our new battalions
even if they joined together to declare us dead:
we're back again wearing our false smile,
we said, exasperated in the face of being forgotten,
while on the island with no palm trees,
there where the stone noses stick out
like triangular designs of sky and salt,
there, in the miniscule navel of the seas,
we leave behind this final purity,
the open space, those astonishing societies
that raise their naked stone, their truth,
in a place where nobody would dare love or live with them,
that's my own cowardice, I bear witness:
I feel suited only to the most temporary
structures, and in this capitol without walls
of light, of salt, of stone and contemplation,
frightened like everybody else, I saw and gave up
the clear light of mythology,
the statues bathed in blue silence.

XX

LA ISLA

De otros lugares (Ceylán, Orinoco, Valdivia)
salí con lianas, con esponjas, con hilos
de la fecundidad, con las enredaderas
y las negras raíces de la humedad terrestre:
de ti, rosa del mar, piedra absoluta,
salgo limpio, vertiendo la claridad del viento:
revivo azul, metálico, evidente.

XX

THE ISLAND

From other places (Ceylon, Orinoco, Valdivia)
I left with lianas, with sponges, with threads
of fertility, with climbing vines
and black roots in the humid earth:
from you, rose of the sea, absolute stone,
I come away clean, shedding the pure light of the wind:
I awaken to life, blue, metallic, obvious.

XXI

LOS HOMBRES

Yo, de los bosques, de los ferrocarriles en invierno,
yo, conservador de aquel invierno,
del barro
en una calle agobiada, miserable,
yo, poeta oscuro, recibí el beso de piedra en mi frente
y se purificaron mis congojas.

XXI

MEN

I, from the forests, from the railroads in winter,
I, preserver of that winter,
of that mud
in the exhausted street, miserable,
I, poet of darkness, received the kiss of stone on my forehead
and my anguish was made pure.

XXII

LA ISLA

Amor, amor, oh separada mía
por tantas veces mar como nieve y distancia,
mínima y misteriosa, rodeada
de eternidad, agradezco
no sólo tu mirada de doncella,
tu blancura escondida, rosa secreta, sino
el resplandor moral de tus estatuas,
la paz abandonada que impusiste en mis manos:
el día detenido en tu garganta.

XXII

THE ISLAND

My love, my love, O my separate one,
for so long sea like snow and distance,
small and mysterious, surrounded
by the infinite, I am thankful
not only for your lovely innocence,
your hidden whiteness, secret rose, but also
for the moral radiance of your statues,
for the forsaken peace you imposed upon my hands:
the day caught inside your throat.

XXIII

LOS HOMBRES

Porque si coincidiéramos allí
como los elefantes moribundos
dispuestos al oxígeno total,
si armados los satisfechos y los hambrientos,
los árabes y los bretones, los de Tehuantepec
y los de Hamburgo, los duros de Chicago y los senegaleses,
todos, si comprendiéramos que allí guardan las llaves
de la respiración, del equilibrio
basados en la verdad de la piedra y del viento,
si así fuera y corrieran las razas despoblándose
las naciones,
si navegáramos en tropel hacia la Isla,
si todos fueran sabios de golpe y acudiéramos
a Rapa Nui, la mataríamos,
la mataríamos con inmensas pisadas, con dialectos,
escupos, batallas, religiones,
y allí también se acabaría el aire,
caerían al suelo las estatuas,
se harían palos sucios las narices de piedra
y todo moriría amargamente.

XXIII

MEN

And if we were to gather there
like dying elephants
exposed to pure oxygen,
if the well-fed and the starving armed themselves,
the Arabs and the Bretons, those from Tehuantepec
and Hamburg, the gangs of Chicago and the Senegalese,
everyone, if only we knew that on the island they guard the keys
to breath, to a sense of balance
based on the truth of stone and wind,
if only it were so and the different races fled
their dwindling nations
and we sailed to the island in thousands of ships,
if suddenly we got smart and made friends
with Rapa Nui, we would only murder her,
we would trample her with big feet, with dialects,
with spittle, battles, religions,
and then the air would run out,
the statues would tumble to the ground,
their stone noses would be evil clubs
and everything would die, bitterly.

LA ISLA

Adiós, adiós, isla secreta, rosa
de purificación, ombligo de oro:
volvemos unos y otros a las obligaciones
de nuestras enlutadas profesiones y oficios.

¡Adíos, que el gran océano te guarde
lejos de nuestra estéril aspereza!
Ha llegado la hora de odiar la soledad:
esconde, isla, las llaves antiguas
bajo los esqueletos
que nos reprocharán hasta que sean polvo
en sus cuevas de piedra
nuestra invasión inútil.

Regresamos. Y este adiós, prodigado y perdido
es uno más, un adiós
sin más solemnidad que la que allí se queda:
la indiferencia inmóvil en el centro del mar:
cien miradas de piedra que miran hacia adentro
y hacia la eternidad del horizonte.

XXIV

THE ISLAND

Goodbye, goodbye, secret island, rose
of purification, navel of gold,
we return, all of us, to the duties
of our mournful professions and occupations.

Goodbye, let the great sea protect you
from our barren brutality!
The time has come to hate solitude:
hide, island, the ancient keys
under the skeletons
who'll taunt us till they're dust
in your caves of stone,
our invasion hopeless.

We are home. And this farewell, squandered and lost,
is just one more, one goodbye
no more solemn than that which lives there:
the immobile indifference surrounded by the ocean:
a hundred stone faces who gaze within
and forever, into the horizon.

ABOUT THE TRANSLATOR

William O'Daly has been translating Spanish lan-
guage poetry for the last ten years, concentrating
on Pablo Neruda's work since 1976. He is assistant
professor at Eastern Washington University, where
he edits the literary magazine *Willow Springs*. Cop-
per Canyon Press published his translation of
Neruda's *Aún (Still Another Day)* in 1984 and a
limited edition of his own poems, *The Whale in the
Web*, in 1979.